Theory Paper Grade 6   2012   A

Duration 3 hours

Candidates should answer all FIVE questions.
Write your answers on this paper – no others will be accepted.
Answers must be written clearly and neatly – otherwise marks may be lost.

TOTAL MARKS
100

1   Answer ONE section only, (a) or (b).

15

EITHER

(a) Indicate ONE chord at each of the places marked * to accompany the following melody. You may do
so by writing roman numerals or any other recognized method of notation between the staves, OR
by writing notes on the staves which provide a proper harmonic structure; but use only ONE of these
methods.

OR

(b) Complete the bass line and add a suitable figured bass as necessary, *from the first beat of bar 3*, at the places marked * in this passage. If you wish to use a ⁵₃ chord, leave the space under the asterisk blank, but ⁵₃ chords *must* be shown when used as part of a ⁶₄ ⁵₃ progression or when chromatic alteration is required.

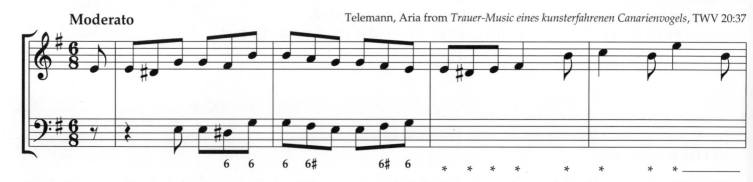

2 Writing for four-part voices (SATB) or keyboard, realize this figured bass.
   Assume that all chords are ⁵₃ unless otherwise shown.

3 EITHER

(a) Continue this opening to form a complete melody for unaccompanied flute. It should end with a modulation to the subdominant and should be between eight and ten bars long. Add performance directions as appropriate and write the complete melody on the staves below.

OR

(b) Continue this opening for unaccompanied cello to make a complete piece of not less than eight bars in length. You may make any modulation or modulations that you wish, or none if you prefer. Add performance directions as appropriate and write the complete melody on the staves below.

Adagio cantabile

4 Look at the extract printed opposite, which is from a piano piece, and then answer the questions below.

25

(a) Identify the chord marked * in bar 10 by writing on the dotted lines below. Use either words or symbols. Indicate the position of the chord, show whether it is major, minor, augmented or diminished, and name the prevailing key.

Bar 10 .... Key .... (4)

(b) Name one similarity and three differences between bar 2 and bar 6.

Similarity .... (1)

Differences 1 .... (1)

2 .... (1)

3 .... (1)

(c) Mark **clearly** on the score, using the appropriate capital letter for identification, one example of each of the following. Also give the bar number(s) of each of your answers. The first answer is given.

From bar 10 onwards

A a melodic interval of a minor 7th in the left-hand part (circle the notes concerned). Bar ...14...

B a Ic–V⁷–I cadence in the dominant key (mark ☐ B ☐ over the notes concerned). Bars .... (2)

C a rising chromatic semitone (augmented unison) in the right-hand part (circle the notes concerned). Bar .... (2)

D a harmonic interval of a diminished 5th in the right-hand part (circle the notes concerned). Bar .... (2)

(d) Write out in full the top right-hand part of bar 13 as you think it should be played.

(3)

(e) Give the full names (e.g. changing note) of the notes of melodic decoration marked **X**, **Y** and **Z**:

X (bar 12, right hand) .... (2)

Y (bar 18, left hand) .... (2)

Z (bar 19, right hand) .... (2)

(f) From the list below, underline the name of the most likely composer of this extract and give a reason for your answer.

       Debussy   Handel   Beethoven   Wagner (1)

Reason: .... (1)

5 Look at the orchestral extract printed on pages 9–10, which is from Liszt's *Héroïde funèbre*, and then answer the questions below.

25

    (a) Name three *non-transposing* standard orchestral instruments, one woodwind and two brass, that do *not* play in this extract.

        Woodwind ....

        Brass .... and ....   (3)

    (b) (i) Write out the parts for clarinets in bars 1–3 as they would sound at concert pitch.

                                                        (3)

      (ii) Write out the part for first horn in bars 3–5 as it would sound at concert pitch.

                                                        (3)

    (c) Give the meaning of:

        senza sord. (e.g. bar 10, second violins) .... (2)

        marziale (bar 11, trumpet) .... (2)

        pizz. (e.g. bar 12, first violins) .... (2)

         (e.g. bar 12, second violins) .... (2)

    (d) Describe fully the numbered and bracketed harmonic intervals *sounding* between:

        1 double basses and first bassoon, bar 1 .... (2)

        2 first and second bassoons, bar 6 .... (2)

    (e) Answer TRUE or FALSE to each of the following statements:

        (i) In bars 5–6 the second violins and the violas sound in unison. .... (2)

        (ii) On the first beat of bar 13, the notes
             form a chord of B♭ major in first inversion. .... (2)

Theory Paper Grade 6   2012   B

Duration 3 hours

TOTAL MARKS
100

Candidates should answer all FIVE questions.
Write your answers on this paper – no others will be accepted.
Answers must be written clearly and neatly – otherwise marks may be lost.

1   Answer ONE section only, (a) or (b).

15

EITHER

(a) Indicate ONE chord at each of the places marked * to accompany the following melody. You may do
so by writing roman numerals or any other recognized method of notation between the staves, OR
by writing notes on the staves which provide a proper harmonic structure; but use only ONE of these
methods.

[Allegretto]   Rameau, Gavotte (adapted)

OR

(b) Complete the bass line and add a suitable figured bass as necessary, *from the second beat of bar 2,* at the places marked * in this passage. If you wish to use a $\frac{5}{3}$ chord, leave the space under the asterisk blank, but $\frac{5}{3}$ chords *must* be shown when used as part of a $\frac{6}{4}\frac{5}{3}$ progression or when chromatic alteration is required.

2 Writing for four-part voices (SATB) or keyboard, realize this figured bass. Assume that all chords are $\frac{5}{3}$ unless otherwise shown.

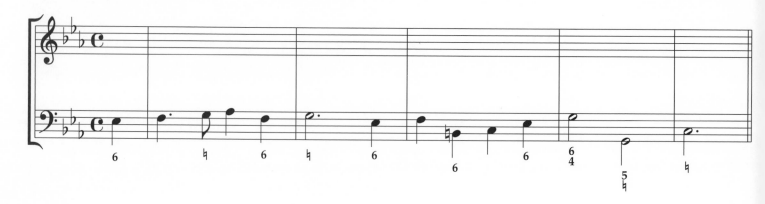

3 EITHER

(a) Continue this opening to form a complete melody for unaccompanied violin. It should end with a modulation to the relative minor and should be between eight and ten bars long. Add performance directions as appropriate and write the complete melody on the staves below.

Adagio cantabile

Boccherini

OR

(b) Continue this opening for unaccompanied oboe to make a complete piece of not less than eight bars in length. You may make any modulation or modulations that you wish, or none if you prefer. Add performance directions as appropriate and write the complete melody on the staves below.

Andante con moto

4 Look at the extract printed opposite, which is from a song, and then answer the questions below.

(a) Mark **clearly** on the score, using the appropriate capital letter for identification, one example of each of the following. Also give the bar number(s) of each of your answers. The first answer is given.

From bar 11 onwards

A   an accented passing note in the vocal part (circle the note concerned).   Bar ....19....

B   two consecutive bars in the piano part that are
immediately repeated (mark ⌐   B   ⌐ over the bars).   Bars .... (2)

C   three grace notes that form a major triad in
second inversion (circle the notes concerned).   Bar .... (2)

D   a lower auxiliary note in the vocal part (circle the note concerned).   Bar .... (2)

(b) Give the meaning of:

Etwas geschwind   .... (4)

⅜ (e.g. bar 1, right-hand piano)   .... (2)

simile (bar 6, left-hand piano)   .... (2)

(c) Identify the chords marked * in bars 13 and 19 by writing on the dotted lines below. Use either words or symbols. For each chord, indicate the position, show whether it is major, minor, augmented or diminished, and name the prevailing key.

Bar 13   ....   Key   .... (4)

Bar 19   ....   Key   .... (4)

(d) Complete the following statement:

The music begins in the key of C major. In bars 7–8 it passes through the key

of .... and in bars 10–11 it passes through the key of .... (2)

(e) From the list below, underline one period during which you think this extract was written.

1600–1700   1700–1800   1800–1900 (1)

5 Look at the orchestral extract printed on pages 17–18, which is from the third movement of Stanford's Symphony No. 7, and then answer the questions below. [25]

(a) Give the meaning of:

Morendo .... (2)

+ (bar 1, horns) .... (2)

(b) (i) Write out the part for clarinet in bars 6–7 as it would sound at concert pitch.

Clarinet

(3)

(ii) Using the blank staves at the foot of page 18, write out the parts for third and fourth horns in bars 8–10 as they would sound at concert pitch and using the given clefs. (4)

(c) Mark **clearly** on the score, using the appropriate capital letter for identification, one example of each of the following. Also give the bar number of each of your answers. The first answer is given.

In bars 1–9

A a dominant pedal note in a brass section lasting for over two bars.   Bars ......2–4......

B a rising chromatic semitone (augmented unison)
in a string part (circle the notes concerned).   Bar .... (2)

C a harmonic interval of a major 7th between
two brass instruments (circle the notes concerned).   Bar .... (2)

D an instruction to the second violins to remove their mutes.   Bar .... (2)

(d) Complete the following statements:

(i) The opening motif played by the clarinet (marked ⌐_____⌐) is later repeated

(not exactly) by the .... in bars .... (2)

(ii) The instruments sounding in unison with the second violins on the first note

of bar 7 are the .... and the .... (2)

(iii) The first bassoon and second violins play the note .... in unison in bar .... (2)

(e) Answer TRUE or FALSE to the following statement:

The smallest harmonic interval between the two bassoon parts is a major 3rd.   .... (2)

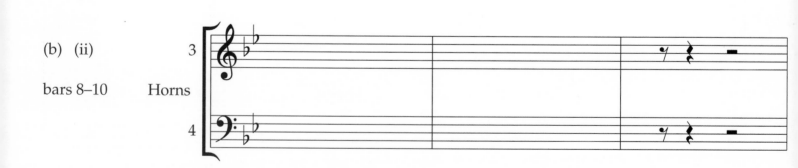

(b) (ii)

bars 8–10   Horns

Theory Paper Grade 6   2012   C

Duration 3 hours

TOTAL MARKS
100

Candidates should answer all FIVE questions.
Write your answers on this paper – no others will be accepted.
Answers must be written clearly and neatly – otherwise marks may be lost.

1 Answer ONE section only, (a) or (b).

15

EITHER

(a) Indicate ONE chord at each of the places marked * to accompany the following melody. You may do
so by writing roman numerals or any other recognized method of notation between the staves, OR
by writing notes on the staves which provide a proper harmonic structure; but use only ONE of these
methods.

OR

(b) Complete the bass line and add a suitable figured bass as necessary, *from the third beat of bar 3*, at the places marked ∗ in this passage. If you wish to use a ⅗ chord, leave the space under the asterisk blank, but ⅗ chords *must* be shown when used as part of a ⁶₄⁵₃ progression or when chromatic alteration is required.

2 Writing for four-part voices (SATB) or keyboard, realize this figured bass. Assume that all chords are ⅗ unless otherwise shown.

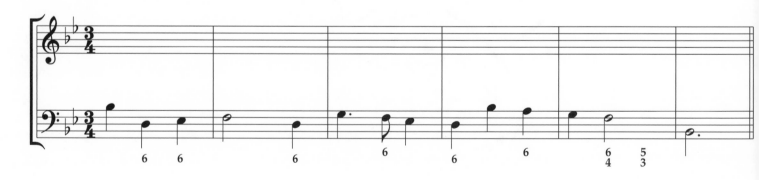

3 EITHER

(a) Continue this opening to form a complete melody for unaccompanied violin. It should end with a modulation to the relative major and should be between eight and ten bars long. Add performance directions as appropriate and write the complete melody on the staves below.

Presto non assai

Brahms (adapted)

OR

(b) Continue this opening for unaccompanied trombone to make a complete piece of not less than eight bars in length. You may make any modulation or modulations that you wish, or none if you prefer. Add performance directions as appropriate and write the complete melody on the staves below.

Allegro giocoso

4 Look at the extract printed opposite, which is from a piano piece by Reinecke, and then answer the questions below. `[25]`

(a) Give the meaning of *calando* (bar 32). .... (2)

(b) Name one similarity and two differences between bars 9–10 and 28–29.

　Similarity .... (1)

　Differences 1 .... (1)

　　　　　　2 .... (1)

(c) Identify the chords marked ⌈ * ⌉ in bars 8 and 20 by writing on the dotted lines below. Use either words or symbols. For each chord, indicate the position, show whether it is major, minor, augmented or diminished, and name the prevailing key in bar 20.

　Bar 8 .... Key: F major (3)

　Bar 20 .... Key .... (4)

(d) Mark **clearly** on the score, using the appropriate capital letter for identification, one example of each of the following. Also give the bar number of each of your answers. The first answer is given.

　In bars 9–20

　A an acciaccatura (grace note) in the right-hand part (circle the note concerned).   Bar ...11....

　B a melodic interval of a diminished 3rd in the right-hand part (circle the notes concerned).   Bar .... (2)

　C an augmented triad in the left-hand part (circle the notes concerned).   Bar .... (2)

　From bar 21 onwards

　D a falling chromatic semitone (augmented unison) in the left-hand part (circle the notes concerned).   Bar .... (2)

　E an interrupted cadence in the tonic key.   Bar .... (2)

　F a lower auxiliary note in the right-hand part (circle the note concerned).   Bar .... (2)

(e) Write out in full the right-hand part of bar 4 as you think it should be played.

(3)

5 Look at the extract printed opposite, which is from an opera, and then answer the questions below.

(a) Give the meaning of:

Lent .... (2)

tr~~~~~~ (bar 1, timpani) .... (2)

à 2 (bar 7, flutes) .... (2)

(b) (i) Write out the parts for clarinets in bars 2–3 as they would sound at concert pitch.

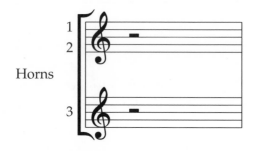

(4)

(ii) Write out the parts for horns in bar 7 as they would sound at concert pitch.

(3)

(c) Complete the following statement:

There is syncopation in a part for a transposing double-reed instrument in

bar .... and bar ...., and also in a part for a single-reed instrument in bar .... (3)

(d) Describe fully the numbered and bracketed harmonic intervals *sounding* between:

1 cellos and first bassoon, bar 4 .... (2)

2 first clarinet and first oboe, bar 6 .... (2)

3 cellos and cor anglais, bar 10 .... (2)

(e) Answer TRUE or FALSE to the following statement:

The second oboe and first clarinet parts cross in bar 3. .... (2)

(f) From the list below, underline the name of the most likely composer of this extract.

Brahms   Handel   Elgar   Debussy   (1)

BLANK PAGE

Theory Paper Grade 6   2012   S

Duration 3 hours

Candidates should answer all FIVE questions.
Write your answers on this paper – no others will be accepted.
Answers must be written clearly and neatly – otherwise marks may be lost.

TOTAL MARKS
100

1 Answer ONE section only, (a) or (b).

15

EITHER

(a) Indicate ONE chord at each of the places marked ∗ to accompany the following melody. You may do so by writing roman numerals or any other recognized method of notation between the staves, OR by writing notes on the staves which provide a proper harmonic structure; but use only ONE of these methods.

OR

(b) Complete the bass line and add a suitable figured bass as necessary, *from the third beat of bar 3*, at the places marked ∗ in this passage. If you wish to use a ⅝ chord, leave the space under the asterisk blank, but ⅝ chords *must* be shown when used as part of a ⁶₄⁵ progression or when chromatic alteration is required.

Handel, Flute Sonata in G (adapted)

2 Writing for four-part voices (SATB) or keyboard, realize this figured bass. Assume that all chords are ⅝ unless otherwise shown.

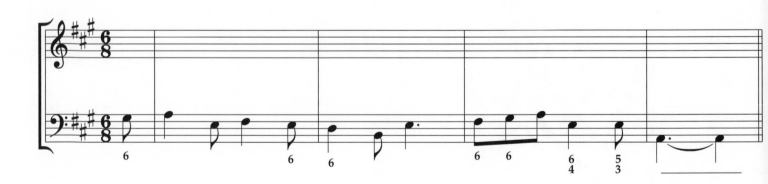

3 EITHER

20

(a) Continue this opening to form a complete melody for unaccompanied flute. It should end with a modulation to the dominant and should be between eight and ten bars long. Add performance directions as appropriate and write the complete melody on the staves below.

Tempo di minuetto

Franz Danzi

OR

(b) Continue this opening for unaccompanied cello to make a complete piece of not less than eight bars in length. You may make any modulation or modulations that you wish, or none if you prefer. Add performance directions as appropriate and write the complete melody on the staves below.

Allegro deciso

4 Look at the extract printed opposite, which is from a piece for flute and keyboard, and then answer the questions below.

(a) Give the full names (e.g. changing note) of the notes of melodic decoration marked **X**, **Y** and **Z** in the flute part of bars 2–4:

X (bar 2) .... (2)

Y (bar 3) .... (2)

Z (bar 4) .... (2)

(b) Identify the chords marked * in bars 3 and 6 by writing on the dotted lines below. Use either words or symbols. For each chord, indicate the position, show whether it is major, minor, augmented or diminished, and name the prevailing key.

Bar 3 .... Key .... (4)

Bar 6 .... Key .... (4)

(c) Write out in full the flute part of bar 11 as you think it should be played.

(3)

(d) Complete the following statement:

From bar 8 onwards, the largest
melodic interval in the flute part is a(n) .... (2)

(e) Mark **clearly** on the score, using the appropriate capital letter for identification, one example of each of the following. Also give the bar number of each of your answers. The first answer is given.

From bar 6 onwards

A   a half-bar in which the flute part is
     lower than the top right-hand keyboard part.   Bar .....8....

B   a dominant 7th chord in root position (V⁷a) in the tonic key.   Bar .... (2)

C   a V–I progression in the subdominant key.   Bar .... (2)

(f) From the list below, underline the name of the most likely composer of this extract and give a reason for your choice.

        Chopin   Verdi   J. S. Bach   Mozart   (1)

Reason: .... (1)

5 Look at the extract printed opposite, which is from the Finale of Lennox Berkeley's
Divertimento in B flat, Op. 18, and then answer the questions below.

(a) Give the meaning of:

Un poco meno vivo .... (3)

unis. (e.g. bar 4, cellos) .... (2)

a 2 (bar 11, flutes) .... (2)

(b) (i) Write out the part for clarinet in bars 6–7 as it would sound at concert pitch.

(4)

(ii) Write out the part for horn in bar 8 as it would sound at concert pitch.

(2)

(c) Describe fully the numbered and bracketed harmonic intervals on the first beat of each of the
following bars, *sounding* between:

1 cellos and bassoon, bar 4 .... (2)

2 double basses and horn, bar 5 .... (2)

3 first violins and clarinet, bar 11 .... (2)

(d) Complete the following statement:

The second violins have to play an open string in bar(s) .... and the violas have to (2)

play an open string in bar .... (2)

(e) Answer TRUE or FALSE to the following statement:

In bar 4, the notes played by the bassoon and horn *sound* an octave apart. .... (2)

Music Theory Past Papers 2012

Four separate papers from ABRSM's 2012 Theory exams for Grade 6

- Essential practice material for all ABRSM Theory exam candidates
- Model answers also available

Support material for ABRSM Theory exams

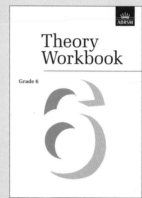
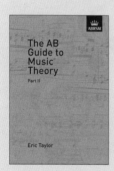

ABRSM
24 Portland Place
London W1B 1LU
United Kingdom

www.abrsm.org

ABRSM is the exam board of the Royal Schools of Music. We are committed to actively supporting high-quality music-making, learning and development throughout the world, and to producing the best possible resources for music teachers and students.

Published by ABRSM (Publishing) Ltd, a wholly owned subsidiary of ABRSM
Cover by Kate Benjamin & Andy Potts
Printed in England by Halstan & Co. Ltd, Amersham, Bucks

ABRSM THEORY OF MUSIC EXAM
2012 GR 6
9781848494534
BP   E £3.95
09/15
4956289/00

ISBN 978-1-84849-453-4

9 781848 494534